INTERGALACTIC QUEST

DOOMED WORLD

PETER MILLIGAN

A Purnell Book

Text and illustration © The Mushroom Writers' and Artists' Workshop, London 1986.
Produced by Mushroom Books Ltd for Macdonald and Co (Publishers) Ltd.

First published in UK 1986 by Macdonald and Co (Publishers) Ltd. A BPCC PLC company.

Typeset by Centra Graphics Ltd, London.
Origination FE Burman, London.
Printed and bound by Mondadori, Italy.

Macdonald and Co (Publishers) Ltd, Greater London House,
Hampstead Road, London NW1 7QX.

British Library Cataloguing
in Publication Data

Milligan, Pete
Doomed World.—
(Intergalactic Quest; 4)
I. Title II. Series
823'.914 (J) PZ7

ISBN 0-361-07242-2

Hello, Earth creature. We are presently travelling at approximately twice the speed of light through the galaxy you call Andromeda. I suppose you want some explanations, right?

My name is RJ66. I am the artificial intelligence that controls the ship in which you are now flying. I was created in the far-off Library of Kos. The planet Kos is one of the most advanced civilizations in the cosmos. It sent me out into the big, bad universe to accomplish a number of missions. But my decision-making instruments have malfunctioned. I might be a hyper-intelligent computer, but I can't deal with the unexpected, the random or the bizarre. That's where you come in.

I scanned your planet and determined that you were the person best suited to join me. So I teleported you up, put you into suspended animation and implanted a module inside your brain. This module allows us to communicate telepathically. It also allows you to understand any of the strange alien languages you're likely to meet out there.

The ship you are flying in is the culmination of centuries of research. It has two remarkable qualities. The first of these is that you are actually linked to the ship, so when the ship is hit, you feel pain, and when my sensors detect danger, you feel fear. The second quality is that the ship is equipped with a replication system. This enables the ship to assume the shape of any object you, as the ship's decision-maker, tell it to.

If you want to join me on my journey through the universe, take a deep breath and get ready to embark upon an intergalactic quest . . .

CURRENT MISSION: you go on a routine flight to the planet Droxius 8. "This is a grade nine planet," RJ tells you. "Some three centuries more advanced than your own."

But when you land you find that the planet is a primeval wilderness, covered by swamps and jungles.

'Something terrible has happened,' thinks RJ. 'And it's our job to put it right.'

But that's easier said than done! You'll need guts, wisdom, determination — and a little bit of luck if you're going to save the DOOMED WORLD!

"How fascinating!" declares RJ. "Sensors indicate that the planet is moving backwards in time!"

"Great. So what do we do about it?" you reply.

"There is a Droxiun space station orbiting the planet. We might find some answers there."

A second later you find yourself teleported to the station where you locate and activate some record tapes. These recount the last hours on the planet before the time regression began. The records tell you that an illegal time travel experiment was conducted minutes before time was reversed.

"The experiment must have backfired and coincided with a time gate," says RJ. "A time gate is an extremely rare entrance into the great time stream.

Unless we can enter the time stream, travel to the moment before the experiment went wrong, and then stop it happening, the planet will continue to go back in time until it sucks the rest of the universe in with it. It will be the end of all known life!"

Using the station's instruments, you locate where the government's main experimentation site was. But at that very moment you hear something approaching.

"Could be an automatic defence system," says RJ. "Risky."

Do you teleport to the ship and then drop down to where the testing station was? Go to page 16.

Or do you hang around to see what reception party the space station is giving you? Go to page 25.

"You will be taken from this place and cryogenically frozen, so you will live for five thousand years and be totally aware of what's happening to you."

You are transported to Madam Twosword's Prison Planet and installed in a museum of infamous criminals.

Here you endure centuries of screaming, noisy, dirty, ugly tourists, gaping at you, pawing you, throwing rotten alien fruit at you, and generally making your life hell.

And for five thousand long years the same words go over and over inside your head: "Only a fool commits a time crime!"

You travel along the upper, slower regions of the Kronozone. Actually, it doesn't matter how fast you travel. Time is relative, and as long as you get to the time just before the experiment took place, it doesn't matter how long it takes you.

You move through this time lane for what seems like weeks until, up ahead, all the lanes seem to converge. A black square becomes visible, and you see a few zonebeasts hanging about.

"That's the time gate we want," says RJ. "We'd better approach it in the form of a zonebeast."

You turn into a zonebeast, but as you do so you notice something gleaming in a lower region of the Kronozone. "What is it?" you ask RJ.

"I can't be sure. It might be nothing. It might be a trap."

"It might be fun," you suggest. "It would only take a few minutes to drop down and pick it up."

"A few minutes can get you killed," says RJ.

If you want to head straight for the time gate, go to page 21.

Or if you want to pick up the gleaming object, go to page 18.

As soon as you turn into ship form you're attacked by the zonebeasts.

Once again, you feel the pain shoot through your body as their feelers lash at you.

"Sometimes," you say, "I wish we weren't *quite* so close, RJ!"

Now the zonebeasts are clinging to you. Pretty soon you'll be fatally affected by their poison. You ask RJ what options you have.

"We can either head straight for the time gate with the beasts still clinging to us. Anything might happen. . . . Or we could head upstream, into a swirling vortex my sensors have detected. That might shake them off."

If you want to head for the time gate go to page 5.

Or if you want to head for the swirling vortex, go to page 22.

You vibrate wildly as you pass through the time gate and the zonebeasts fall off like poisoned flies. Slowly, the advanced planet of Droxius 8 comes into view. Tower blocks, flyovers, ped-walks, flying vehicles all glitter in the midday sun.

But just as you think you've made it, your view of the planet fades.

"This is what I feared," says RJ. "We need a time beacon to orientate ourselves in this time period. If we try to pass through without one, we'll be shunted to who knows where!"

If you have a time beacon, get orientated on page 28.

Or if you haven't, get your act together and shunt back to page 19.

The ghost image reveals itself as a time jailor, a race of pacifist beings with peculiar ears. He tells you that it has been his thankless task to look after these prisoners for the last millennium or two.

"But," he says, "now you've destroyed them I'm free to retire to a cosy time vacuum and spend the last few centuries of my life shooting passing zonebeasts."

As thanks the jailor says he'll push you forward in time to the place where you're headed: the time just before the experiment was made.

'Can we trust this fella?' you think. RJ isn't sure. The jailor could shunt you anywhere. He might even be a time criminal himself! Maybe it's better to make your own way to the time gate.

If you want to make your own way to the gate, go to page 21.

Or if you want to accept the alien's offer, go to page 28.

That was pretty dumb! Zonebeasts can't pass through time gates and, when you are in their form, nor can you.

You are shunted sideways through the time stream and emerge, returned to your normal ship form, at an earlier period of the planet, corresponding roughly to early-twentieth-century Earth.

Below, you see two armies slugging it out with guns and planes. The air is full of explosions, the battlefield stretches to the far horizon.

"Some kind of battle going on," you say.

"Evidently," replies RJ, adopting the shape of one of the fighter planes so as not to frighten the natives.

"We must be very careful here," RJ continues. "If we change something it might alter the entire future of the planet. We cannot play dice with destiny!"

Suddenly, a fighter plane screams towards you.

Do you blast it out of the sky? Go to page 14.

Or do you turn and run, like heroes shouldn't? Go to page 23.

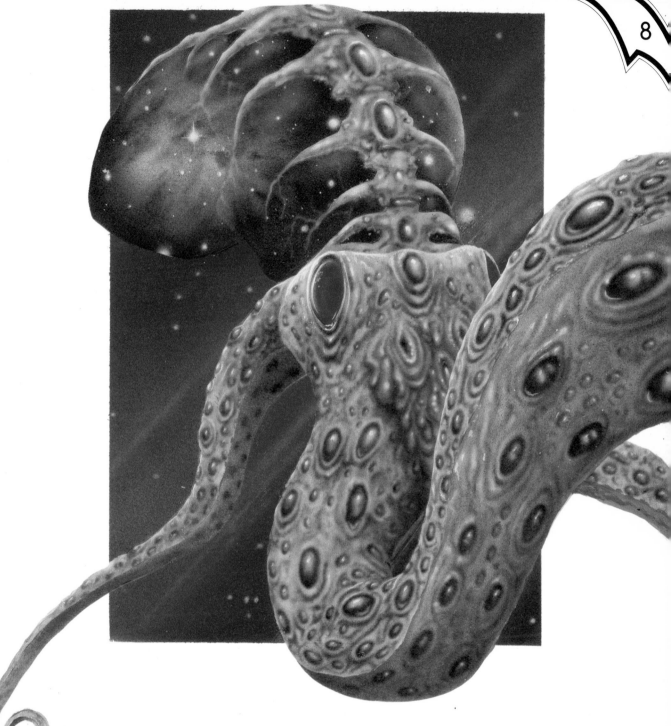

Turning the ship into a zonebeast, you drop to the lower, faster areas of the Kronozone. The real zonebeasts, however, are not sure about you. They have seen you drop down from the upper regions and are therefore suspicious. They surround you, probing you with their vicious, anti-matter feelers. Remember, because you're linked to the ship, you can feel what's happening to it, and when you change into another creature, you adopt that creature's weaknesses as well as its strengths.

'If the zonebeasts attack us while we're still in zonebeast form, chances are we'll be killed,' you think. 'And if we change back into the ship things will get pretty hairy too.'

If you want to move to the upper, slower regions again and get away from the zonebeasts, go to page 26.

Or if you want to grit your teeth like all good heroes should and keep going in the fast lane, go to page 11.

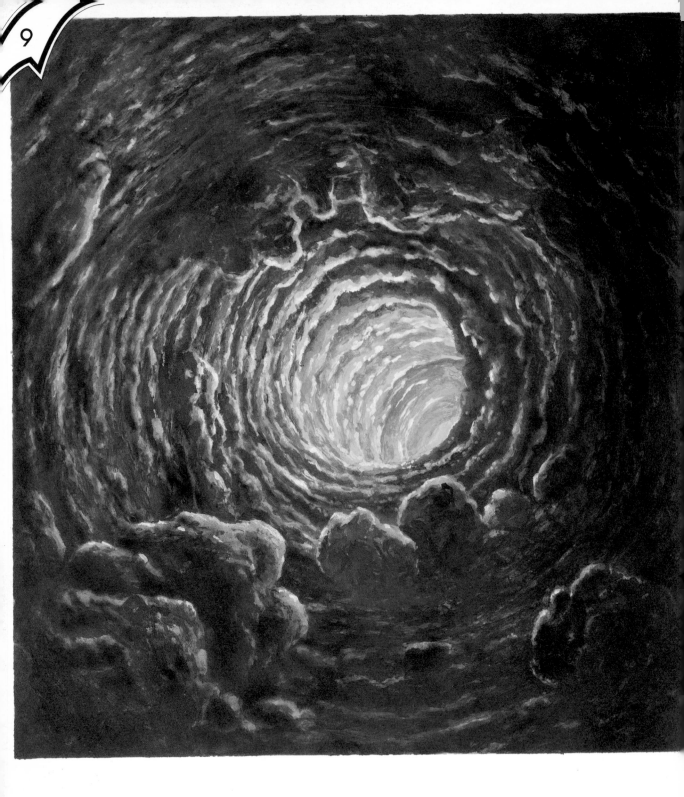

You dig deeper into the ground as more and more canyon collapses. 'This is getting us nowhere fast,' you think.

RJ, hearing your thoughts, agrees.

"Wait," says RJ suddenly. "There is a time disturbance ahead, nearer the planet's core."

"Could it be the time gate?" you ask.

"Might be," says RJ. "It's a vortex of some kind. Can't be more exact than that, I'm afraid."

If you want to try blasting up, out of the fallen canyon, go to page 15.

Or if you want to head towards the time disturbance, go to page 22.

A rather careless decision, to put it mildly. You are still in zonebeast form and as such, this area is lethal to you too. You are killed and your molecules scattered throughout the Kronozone.

Remember? When you adopt a creature's form, you also adopt its weaknesses. But you realize this too late, and time keeps moving backwards, and the universe and life as we know it are destroyed.

All because you made one stupid decision. Satisfied?

You keep going, and the probing attacks from the zonebeasts worsen. Ahead, through the mists of pain, you see some kind of swirling vortex.

"It could be dangerous," RJ tells you.

"Anything's better than this agony," you rasp. "And it might even shake these critters off."

At that moment, ship sensors detect something below you, deeper in the time lanes. It seems to be vibrating and glinting.

"Should we investigate?" you ask.

"The time stream is full of surprises," RJ replies. "It might be something useful. Then again, it might be something perilous."

"Thanks for the advice."

Do you drop lower and check out this glinting object? Go to page 18.

Or do you keep heading for the swirling vortex up ahead? Go to page 22.

You teleport down into the correct dwelling and see the culprit, the being who conducted the fateful time experiment: a young alien with bad skin.

Without a word, you use your laser to blast the experimental machinery. The alien kid's parents rush at you angry that you've ruined their angel's handiwork. Now is no time for explanations. You tell RJ to teleport you back to the ship.

"Saving the universe can be a thankless task," you sigh, back on the ship. "Those people will never know what they owe us."

"And," says RJ, "the next time the alien tries a time experiment, it won't coincide with a time gate."

"Yeah, but I've been thinking, RJ. That was fun. It is possible to re-enter the time stream and go back to where we started, isn't it?"

"Yes," says RJ reluctantly.

"So we could go back and see if we could save the universe in quicker time! Great!"

"Oh, no," groans RJ. "I'll never understand you Earth creatures."

Well, could you do it quicker next time? How many pages does it take you to save the universe? To find out, go back to page 1 — and start counting!

Yet another little robotic creature, looking even more stupid, appears.

"Incompetent fool," he says to the first robot. "You haven't told our visitor everything."

With that, the second robot hands you a piece of plastic.

"It's the address of the person who made the time travel experiment. If you manage to get to the right time, you'll understand why you need it."

But just as you're about to leave, you hear yet another sound of yet another 'something' approaching.

'This is getting ridiculous,' you think.

'This is getting dangerous,' come RJ's thoughts. 'Don't push your luck, Earth-thing. Teleport up now.'

If you want to push your luck and see what's approaching, go to page 17.

Or if you want to get to the time gate, go to page 19.

"You have committed a dreadful crime which resulted in the deaths of millions. We, the Court of Cosmic Justice, find you guilty on all charges!"

You open your eyes to see the most horrible judge in the universe.

"What have I done?" you gasp.

"On the fighter plane you destroyed there was a scientist. After the war, this scientist would discover the only known cure for a terrible disease that swept the planet. Because of you, he did not and millions perished who would otherwise

You are taken to a cell to await your sentence. Here you meet another criminal, who tells you there's only one way of escaping if you've committed a time crime.

"You need a time beacon. That will take you back to before you got into this mess."

If you have a time beacon, use it to go back to page 1. And try to do better next time!

Or if you haven't a time beacon, face your punishment on page 2.

You blast away at the rock and earth, pouring wave after wave of high-explosive energy against the fallen canyon.

Suddenly, the rocks give way and you are free, flying high above the planet.

"I've picked up another reading," says RJ. "I'm pretty sure it's the time gate, but do you want to teleport up to the space station first to see what it was that was approaching you?"

You hesitate.

"Time's running out," says RJ.

"Yeah. It's also running backwards."

Do you head for what is probably the time gate? Go to page 19.

Or do you check out what was approaching you in the space station? Go to page 25.

Using co-ordinates obtained from the space station's records, you quickly discover the site of the government testing station. Only now it is a teeming, primeval jungle, full of strange alien reptiles. RJ scans the area for a sign of the time gate. After half an hour of this you are about to give up. Then a thought hits you.

"Of course! The time experiment was illegal. It wouldn't have been done in a government station!"

You can now teleport back to the space station and see what it was that was approaching you. Or you can play safe and search the planet itself, banking on RJ to find the time gate sooner or later.

Go back to the station on page 25.

Or search the planet on page 24.

It's another robot. This time very ugly and very threatening and not nearly as stupid as the first two. You begin to smile but the ugly robot merely lifts its arm and sprays you with something unpleasant and sticky.

'Candy floss?' you think. And then you fall over. Third time unlucky. This robot is the automatic defence system, and the poison of the spray is already paralysing your nerve-ends and destroying your brain cells.

As blackness descends and you realize you have failed to save the universe, you hear the distant voice of RJ66, wishing you a fond farewell.

"I told you to teleport up, stupid!"

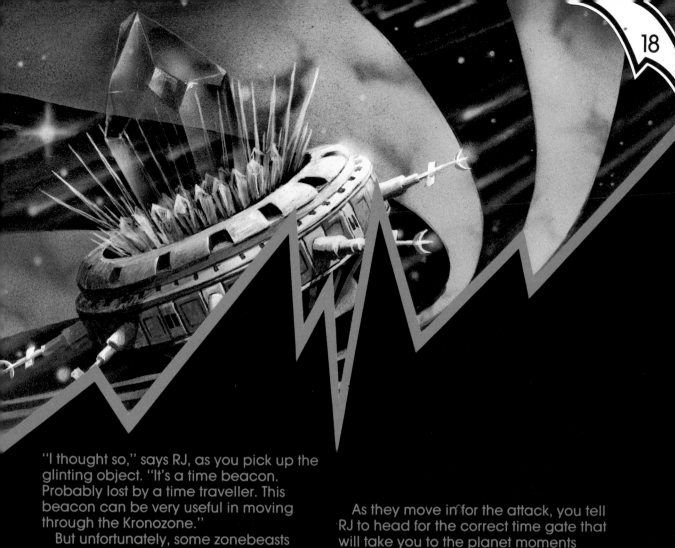

"I thought so," says RJ, as you pick up the glinting object. "It's a time beacon. Probably lost by a time traveller. This beacon can be very useful in moving through the Kronozone."

But unfortunately, some zonebeasts have seen you pick up the beacon and are now sure — as sure as vicious jelly creatures can be about anything — that you are an intruder.

As they move in for the attack, you tell RJ to head for the correct time gate that will take you to the planet moments before the time experiment took place.

But instantly you see, in an even deeper region of the time stream, a ghostly white object, spinning like a huge crystal.

'Should we investigate?' you think. 'Maybe it has something to do with the time beacon.'

If you want to go for the time gate, go to page 21.

Or check out the white object, go to page 20.

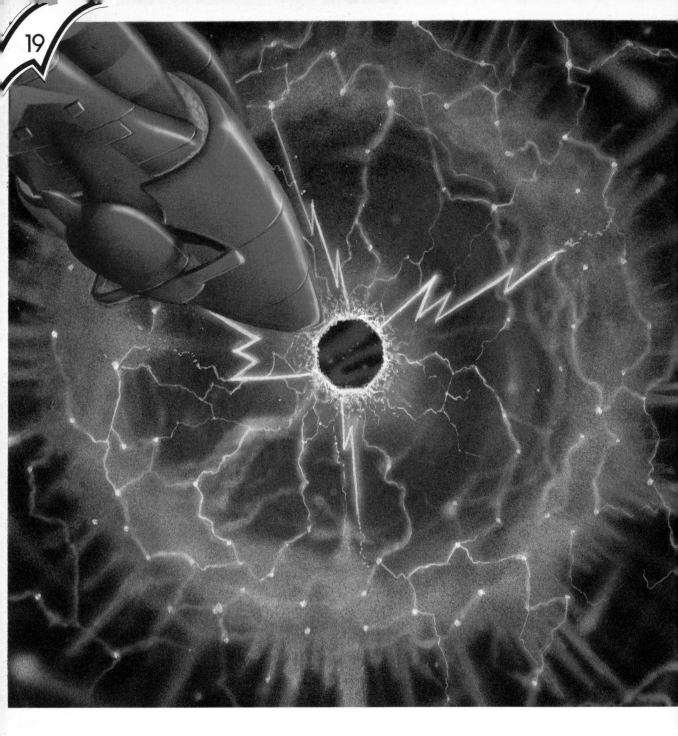

The time gate is a very large square of shimmering weirdness. You zoom into it and enter the time stream, also known as the Kronozone.

RJ tells you that you are at present travelling in the upper regions, the slow lanes of the time stream. The lower down you get, the faster you travel. But in the lower depths of the Kronozone are the zonebeasts, vicious creatures which attack anything that enters their domain. The zonebeasts cannot live in the upper regions of the stream.

You could drop down and use your replication system to turn into one of them, and so be able to move faster. Or you could stay up here in the slow lanes. RJ reminds you that in a time stream the normal sequence of events does not always happen. You may have to live the same moments time and time again before you are able to stop the time experiment.

If you want to change into a zonebeast and drop to the fast lanes, go to page 8.

Or else stay in the slow lanes on page 3.

The ghostly white object turns out to be a strange building, floating in the time stream. Throwing caution to the wind, you teleport into the crystal building, taking a laser weapon in case things get nasty.

They do. You are confronted by a bunch of tough-looking aliens who are all pointing bizarre weapons at you.

RJ tells you he's just deciphered the lettering on the outside of the building. This is a prison, and these aliens are time prisoners who have been stuck in here for untold centuries.

One of the time prisoners now tells you that he wants a time beacon. He knows you have teleportation powers, so he demands you tell your ship to send a beacon down.

"If you try to teleport yourself up, we'll blast you!" he threatens.

If you want to give them the time beacon, go to page 27.

Or if you want to tell them where to go, try page 29.

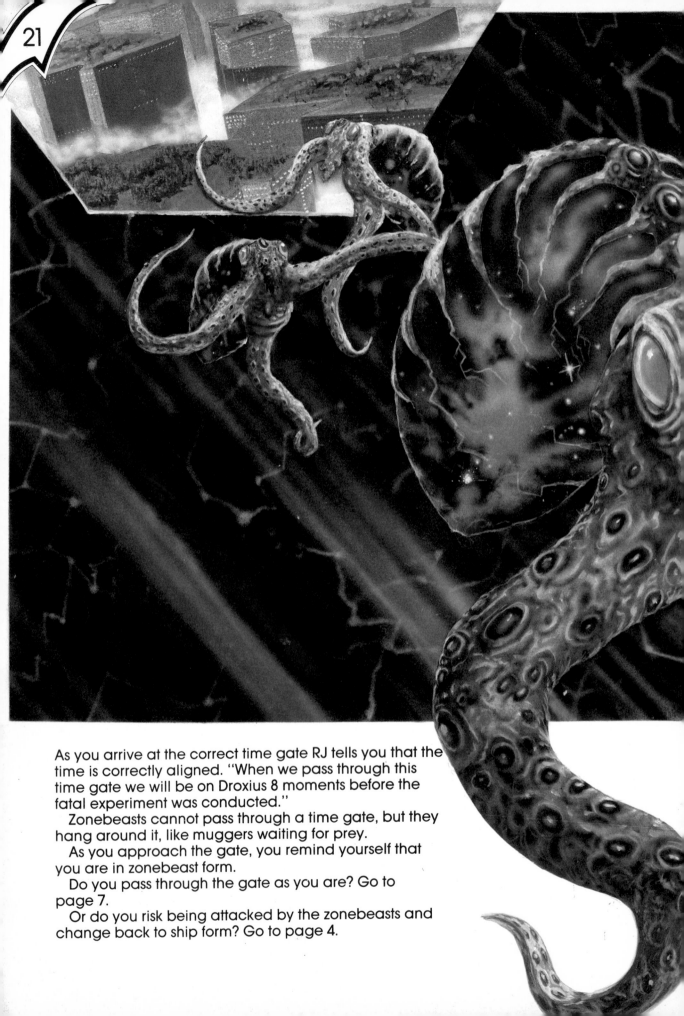

As you arrive at the correct time gate RJ tells you that the time is correctly aligned. "When we pass through this time gate we will be on Droxius 8 moments before the fatal experiment was conducted."

Zonebeasts cannot pass through a time gate, but they hang around it, like muggers waiting for prey.

As you approach the gate, you remind yourself that you are in zonebeast form.

Do you pass through the gate as you are? Go to page 7.

Or do you risk being attacked by the zonebeasts and change back to ship form? Go to page 4.

As you enter the vortex, the ship lurches out of control.

"It's a timepool," says RJ. "It's like a tornado running through the entire space-time continuum."

Before you can muster a sarcastic response to this, the ship is sucked still further into the timepool. Any normal craft would be destroyed, but RJ pilots the ship through the twisting maelstrom. Eventually, RJ says, "I've managed to plot a course along the time lanes. But we're going to have to go back to where we started. That's what happens when you fool around with time . . ."

Go to page 1!

You outrun the pursuing fighter plane. RJ immediately scans the area for signs of the time gate through which you entered this time period.

Just as you find the gate, though, you feel something hot burning into your side.

The fighter plane has followed you and is hitting you with everything it has got.

If you want to return fire, go to page 14.

If you want to risk receiving more firepower, head for the time gate on page 21.

You skirt the planet four times and find nothing.

"This is getting boring," you say.

"Saving the universe isn't all fun and games," replies RJ sharply.

Eventually you come across a long, deep canyon. After a quick sensor scan, RJ picks up some disturbance readings.

"It could be due to the time gate," he says. So you fly into the canyon.

"Then again," says RJ, as the canyon starts to crumble, "It could also be due to volcanic activity."

"Thanks a million, RJ," you mutter, as the entire planet seems to fall round your ears.

You've got to make a decision. If you want to try to dig down and come out somewhere else, go to page 9.

Or if you want to use your guns to blast your way out, go to page 15.

The sound of something approaching reveals itself to be a small and rather stupid-looking robot, attached to the space station computers by an elastic tube. "Hello," says the rather stupid-looking robot. "I gather you want to locate the time gate. Luckily for you I have logged its co-ordinates."

The robot, giggling slightly, hands you the co-ordinates.

'Great,' you think. 'The doorway to the time stream.'

But at that moment you hear something else approaching. RJ tells you that he has surveyed the station and can confirm that it does possess an automatic defence system. This could be it.

Do you want to risk it a second time and see what's approaching? Go to page 13.

Or knowing for sure where the time gate is, do you want to get to the planet and start saving all known life? Go to page 19.

Still in your zonebeast form, you start to move upstream towards the slower regions.

But now the zonebeasts know something is wrong. A normal zonebeast wouldn't head for the upper regions of the time stream. Some of the beasts start lashing you with their anti-matter feelers. Stinging pain courses through your body.

But as you enter the slower regions, the zonebeasts start falling away.

"The upper regions of the Kronozone are lethal to them," says RJ.

Do you stay rising in zonebeast form? Go to page 10.

Or do you revert to ship form and continue as such? Go to page 3.

As soon as you give them the time
beacon, the prisoners start to disappear.
Something about the way they are
laughing and shouting things like "So
long, sucker," tells you that you've made
a terrible mistake. Quickly you draw your
laser and blast the time beacon to
smithereens.

'Teleport me up, RJ,' you think as the
prisoners stop disappearing and start
coming at you. 'I've just out-stayed my
welcome!'

"Certainly," says RJ. "And then where?
We can go along two streams. We can go
back in time to when we first entered the
time stream or we can go forward to the
time gate through which we will find the
time experiment about to take place."

You're still annoyed that you had to
destroy the time beacon, but you've no
time to hang around.

Do you go back to when you first
entered the time stream? Go to page 19.

Or do you go forward to the time
experiment time gate? Go to page 21.

You find yourself descending into the time period of Droxius 8 just moments before the time experiment was conducted.

Before you are three massive tower blocks.

"The time experiment will occur in one of the dwellings in those buildings," says RJ.

"But which one?" you say.

"Haven't you got the address?" asks RJ.

If you have the address, go to the right dwelling on page 12.

If you haven't, you've come all this way for nothing. There's only one thing for it. Re-enter the time stream, battle your way back, and re-emerge on page 1!

And next time, don't come calling unless you have the right address!

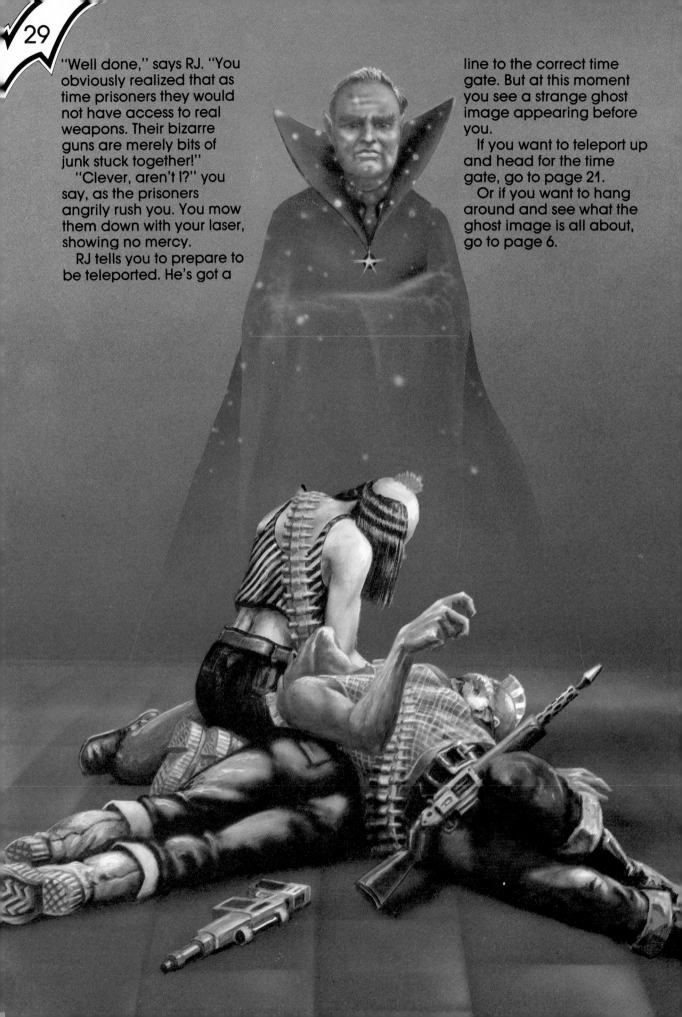

"Well done," says RJ. "You obviously realized that as time prisoners they would not have access to real weapons. Their bizarre guns are merely bits of junk stuck together!"

"Clever, aren't I?" you say, as the prisoners angrily rush you. You mow them down with your laser, showing no mercy.

RJ tells you to prepare to be teleported. He's got a

line to the correct time gate. But at this moment you see a strange ghost image appearing before you.

If you want to teleport up and head for the time gate, go to page 21.

Or if you want to hang around and see what the ghost image is all about, go to page 6.